THIS BOOK IS FOR

....

BORN

....

LOTS OF LOVE
FOREVER & ALWAYS

....

On the day you were born

Date: _____   Weight: _____

Day of the week: _____   Length: _____

Time of birth: _____   Eyes: _____

Place of birth: _____   Hair: _____

The person who delivered you: _____

The first people you met: _____

You were very close to being called _____ or _____

Other runner up names: _____

The weather was: _____

The biggest headline in the news was: _____

The number one song was: _____

My favorite song at the moment (& the song you probably heard most in my tummy: _____

My first impressions of you & how I felt Immediately after your birth: _____

The story of bringing you home from the hospital that day:

Here are a few things you should know about your family:

All the things I hope for your future:

The world I want to give you:

Newborn baby memories

Newborn baby memories

Happy Birthday

To my dearest

What we did to celebrate your birthday:

This last year has been:

Some of my fondest memories:

The trips/vacations we took were:

This year you learnt how to:

Things you loved this year:

Things you didn't like as much:

Milestones:

Changes that have happened over the past year:

Things I have learnt about myself this year:

The best advice I can give you at this point in time:

𝄞 *This years most played songs* 🎵

Mine   Yours
☆   ☆

☆   ☆

☆   ☆

☆   ☆

My wishes and hopes for the next year:

Memories

Happy Birthday

2

To my dearest

What we did to celebrate your birthday:

This last year has been:

Some of my fondest memories:

The trips/vacations we took were:

This year you learnt how to:

Things you loved this year:

Things you didn't like as much:

Milestones:

Changes that have happened over the past year:

Things I have learnt about myself this year:

The best advice I can give you at this point in time:

𝄞 *This years most played songs* ♫

Mine	Yours
☆	☆
☆	☆
☆	☆
☆	☆

My wishes and hopes for the next year:

Memories

Happy Birthday

3

To my dearest

What we did to celebrate your birthday:

This last year has been:

Some of my fondest memories:

The trips/vacations we took were:

This year you learnt how to:

Things you loved this year:

Things you didn't like as much:

Milestones:

Changes that have happened over the past year:

Things I have learnt about myself this year:

The best advice I can give you at this point in time:

𝄞 This years most played songs ♫

Mine

☆

☆

☆

☆

Yours

☆

☆

☆

☆

My wishes and hopes for the next year:

Memories

Happy Birthday

4

To my dearest

What we did to celebrate your birthday:

This last year has been:

Some of my fondest memories:

The trips/vacations we took were:

This year you learnt how to:

Things you loved this year:

Things you didn't like as much:

Milestones:

Changes that have happened over the past year:

Things I have learnt about myself this year:

The best advice I can give you at this point in time:

This years most played songs

Mine

☆

☆

☆

☆

Yours

☆

☆

☆

☆

My wishes and hopes for the next year:

Memories

Happy Birthday

5

To my dearest

What we did to celebrate your birthday:

This last year has been:

Some of my fondest memories:

The trips/vacations we took were:

This year you learnt how to:

Things you loved this year:

Things you didn't like as much:

Milestones:

Changes that have happened over the past year:

Things I have learnt about myself this year:

The best advice I can give you at this point in time:

🎼 *This years most played songs* ♫

Mine   Yours
☆   ☆

☆   ☆

☆   ☆

☆   ☆

My wishes and hopes for the next year:

Memories

Happy Birthday

6

To my dearest

What we did to celebrate your birthday:

This last year has been:

Some of my fondest memories:

The trips/vacations we took were:

This year you learnt how to:

Things you loved this year:

Things you didn't like as much:

Milestones:

Changes that have happened over the past year:

Things I have learnt about myself this year:

The best advice I can give you at this point in time:

This years most played songs ♫

Mine

☆

☆

☆

☆

Yours

☆

☆

☆

☆

My wishes and hopes for the next year:

Memories

Happy Birthday

7

To my dearest

What we did to celebrate your birthday:

This last year has been:

Some of my fondest memories:

The trips/vacations we took were:

This year you learnt how to:

Things you loved this year:

Things you didn't like as much:

Milestones:

Changes that have happened over the past year:

Things I have learnt about myself this year:

The best advice I can give you at this point in time:

𝄞 This years most played songs ♫

Mine

Yours

☆

☆

☆

☆

☆

☆

☆

☆

My wishes and hopes for the next year:

Memories

Happy Birthday

8

To my dearest

What we did to celebrate your birthday:

This last year has been:

Some of my fondest memories:

The trips/vacations we took were:

This year you learnt how to:

Things you loved this year:

Things you didn't like as much:

Milestones:

Changes that have happened over the past year:

Things I have learnt about myself this year:

The best advice I can give you at this point in time:

♪ This years most played songs ♫

Mine   Yours
☆   ☆

☆   ☆

☆   ☆

☆   ☆

My wishes and hopes for the next year:

Memories

Happy Birthday

9

To my dearest

What we did to celebrate your birthday:

This last year has been:

Some of my fondest memories:

The trips/vacations we took were:

This year you learnt how to:

Things you loved this year:

Things you didn't like as much:

Milestones:

Changes that have happened over the past year:

Things I have learnt about myself this year:

The best advice I can give you at this point in time:

𝄞 *This years most played songs* ♫

Mine   Yours
☆   ☆

☆   ☆

☆   ☆

☆   ☆

My wishes and hopes for the next year:

Memories

Happy Birthday

10

To my dearest

What we did to celebrate your birthday:

This last year has been:

Some of my fondest memories:

The trips/vacations we took were:

This year you learnt how to:

Things you loved this year:

Things you didn't like as much:

Milestones:

Changes that have happened over the past year:

Things I have learnt about myself this year:

The best advice I can give you at this point in time:

𝄞 *This years most played songs* ♫

Mine

☆

☆

☆

☆

Yours

☆

☆

☆

☆

My wishes and hopes for the next year:

Memories

Happy Birthday

11

To my dearest

What we did to celebrate your birthday:

This last year has been:

Some of my fondest memories:

The trips/vacations we took were:

This year you learnt how to:

Things you loved this year:

Things you didn't like as much:

Milestones:

Changes that have happened over the past year:

Things I have learnt about myself this year:

The best advice I can give you at this point in time:

$\oint$ *This years most played songs* ♫

Mine   Yours
☆   ☆

☆   ☆

☆   ☆

☆   ☆

My wishes and hopes for the next year:

Memories

Happy Birthday

12

To my dearest

What we did to celebrate your birthday:

This last year has been:

Some of my fondest memories:

The trips/vacations we took were:

This year you learnt how to:

Things you loved this year:

Things you didn't like as much:

Milestones:

Changes that have happened over the past year:

Things I have learnt about myself this year:

The best advice I can give you at this point in time:

♪ This years most played songs ♫

Mine | Yours
☆ | ☆
☆ | ☆
☆ | ☆
☆ | ☆

My wishes and hopes for the next year:

Memories

Happy Birthday

13

To my dearest

What we did to celebrate your birthday:

This last year has been:

Some of my fondest memories:

The trips/vacations we took were:

This year you learnt how to:

Things you loved this year:

Things you didn't like as much:

Milestones:

Changes that have happened over the past year:

Things I have learnt about myself this year:

The best advice I can give you at this point in time:

_____
_____
_____
_____
_____
_____

𝄞 *This years most played songs* ♫

Mine   Yours
☆   ☆
☆   ☆
☆   ☆
☆   ☆

My wishes and hopes for the next year:

_____
_____
_____
_____
_____
_____
_____
_____
_____
_____
_____

Memories

Happy Birthday

14

To my dearest

What we did to celebrate your birthday:

This last year has been:

Some of my fondest memories:

The trips/vacations we took were:

This year you learnt how to:

Things you loved this year:

Things you didn't like as much:

Milestones:

Changes that have happened over the past year:

Things I have learnt about myself this year:

The best advice I can give you at this point in time:

This years most played songs ♫

Mine   Yours
☆   ☆
☆   ☆
☆   ☆
☆   ☆

My wishes and hopes for the next year:

Memories

Happy Birthday

15

To my dearest

What we did to celebrate your birthday:

This last year has been:

Some of my fondest memories:

The trips/vacations we took were:

This year you learnt how to:

Things you loved this year:

Things you didn't like as much:

Milestones:

Changes that have happened over the past year:

Things I have learnt about myself this year:

The best advice I can give you at this point in time:

♪ This years most played songs ♫

Mine   Yours

☆   ☆

☆   ☆

☆   ☆

☆   ☆

My wishes and hopes for the next year:

Memories

Happy Birthday

16

To my dearest

What we did to celebrate your birthday:

This last year has been:

Some of my fondest memories:

The trips/vacations we took were:

This year you learnt how to:

Things you loved this year:

Things you didn't like as much:

Milestones:

Changes that have happened over the past year:

Things I have learnt about myself this year:

The best advice I can give you at this point in time:

♪ This years most played songs ♫

Mine	Yours
☆	☆
☆	☆
☆	☆
☆	☆

My wishes and hopes for the next year:

Memories

Happy Birthday

17

To my dearest

What we did to celebrate your birthday:

This last year has been:

Some of my fondest memories:

The trips/vacations we took were:

This year you learnt how to:

Things you loved this year:

Things you didn't like as much:

Milestones:

Changes that have happened over the past year:

Things I have learnt about myself this year:

The best advice I can give you at this point in time:

♪ This years most played songs ♫

Mine   Yours
☆   ☆
☆   ☆
☆   ☆
☆   ☆

My wishes and hopes for the next year:

Memories

Happy Birthday

To my dearest

What we did to celebrate your birthday:

This last year has been:

Some of my fondest memories:

The trips/vacations we took were:

This year you learnt how to:

Things you loved this year:

Things you didn't like as much:

Milestones:

Changes that have happened over the past year:

Things I have learnt about myself this year:

The best advice I can give you at this point in time:

𝄞 *This years most played songs* ♫

Mine   Yours
☆   ☆
☆   ☆
☆   ☆
☆   ☆

My wishes and hopes for the next year:

Now that you are an adult (Kind of)

Be prepared to:

Always keep:

Focus on:

Never:

Always remember:

Be Open to:

Surround yourself with:

I wish you:

One last thing:

Memories

Memories

Memories

Memories

Memories

Memories

Made in the USA
Las Vegas, NV
24 August 2023

76514240R00070